The Lost Kitten

By Annette Smith

Illustrations by Richard Hoit

W0099689

One Saturday morning,
Tom and his grandfather
walked to the park
at the end of the road.

Tom wanted to kick his football
around at the park.

On the way,
they saw a girl.

She was looking for something
in the bushes, by a big tree.

The girl told Tom and his grandfather that she had lost her little grey kitten.

The girl was very upset because the kitten was a present for her birthday.

Tom and his grandfather
helped the girl
look for the kitten.

Suddenly, Tom saw a grey tail
moving in the leaves of the tree.

The little kitten
was clinging to a branch.
It was too scared
to come down.

The girl called to the kitten,
but it stayed in the tree.

Tom held his hand up to the kitten and called to it, too.

Then the kitten climbed slowly down the tree to Tom.